URBAN PREPPER

By Christopher LaVoie

This book is dedicated to Charles, Erika, and Alexis.

Disclaimer:

Any points made in this book that violates local, state or federal laws are presented purely for entertainment purposes.

That being said…read those points twice.

A note from the author to you:

Well done! You have just done something wonderful and rare. I realize this may sound strange, but you have just set yourself far apart from the majority of the world's population. Indeed, you have placed yourself among a unique group of around 10% of the global inhabitants, if that. Outstanding!

What a fantastic feat have you accomplished? What have you done to command such acclaim? You have taken a deep breath, calmly analyzed the realities of the world around you and…made a decision. You are now fully qualified to call yourself…Decisive! While this may sound trivial at first, it is by no means such. It is truthfully the first and foremost trait in what I will explain later to have the "survival mindset."

While 90% of the world's citizens living in highly congested cities and densely packed urban wastelands know they are one flick of the light switch away from saying "uh…now what?", you have put yourself among a much smaller group that wants actually to have an answer to this.
You have decided to learn more about what your options are if that light switch flicker leads to …nothing. No light, no power, no sewer system, no gas, no police, no fire department, no cell phone, etc., etc.

The safety blanket of "society" is far thinner than most realize and the chill in the air is blowing right through it.   We watched as major cities melted into chaos and anarchy during the New

Orleans, Hurricane Katrina aftermath. We witnessed the post "superstorm" scrambling of humanity in the streets of New York City itself. When millions of citizens live within a few square miles of land, they require some basic needs to maintain daily life.

Infrastructure. The loss of sewer systems, fresh water, power blackouts and clogged roadways can bring even the largest cities to a standstill in a matter of hours. You take your 15-minute hot showers for granted. What would you do if the toilet did not refill after that first flush? No hot coffee, no cooked or microwaved breakfast. Refrigerator off. Think yourself through one-morning ritual without power, water, and traversable roadways. Trust me, you are going to need a drink after that assessment.

Food and water. While we pride ourselves as modern, bountiful and fruitful in general, the reality is that cities require a 24-hour inbound stream of food and water supplies to keep the population alive. The occasional rooftop garden or the cleared alley that has given way to a community vegetable-growing co-op may set a positive atmosphere for a neighborhood, but they in no way will provide nourishment for millions of people who have never picked up a shovel or even taken the time to sink their hands deep into the rich soil.

One of my favorite lines the Joker used; "these people with their morals when the chips are down, they'll eat each other." No truer statement has been said, as proven in survival scenarios throughout time. Plane crashes on frozen mountain tops or ship's crews set adrift in the wide expanse of ocean.

Security. As a child, I remember the days or, frightfully, the weeks that major cities would endure when the local law enforcement would protest a criminal case outcome or an officer's indictment with the "blue flu." This was a department-wide sick day that would leave the streets devoid of police officers and patrol cars.

The days would start as always, folks stopping for stop lights on the way to work in the morning and businesses opening their doors for a day of commerce. Every time, the day would end in drivers ignoring any semblance of traffic law. Shoppers would turn into looters and vandals as the city slipped into a moray of violence and burning shops.

When the police can not respond, it is no different than when they refuse to. You have to protect yourself and those you care about. Honestly, is it that different than any other day? Call 911 right now and listen to the "all lines are busy" recording…good luck with that.

Shelter. You sit in hours of traffic on your way home, but you know just a few miles, and a key turn away is your warm and dry apartment. Your favorite seat, Netflix, dinner, and a cold beer. A soft bed to crawl into later in the evening. What if you parked at your building and found hundreds of people using the garage levels as shelter? Your door kicked in and another family in your home? Your home…the one you pay for, work for, expect to be there.

Now take that family's position. You find out that your entire neighborhood is closed off, dozens of square blocks surrounded by the national guard. A dirty bomb smuggled across the Mexican border was detonated and you will never, as of that moment, set foot in your home or neighborhood again. It is quarantined, and the half life of the radioactive material is…decades at best.

You walk with your family if you are with them. A rare situation if this all goes down at say … 1030 am on a Tuesday. There are a few tents, packed. Porta-potties are delivered to the local parking lot / temporary tent community. You will not let your children sleep on the concrete, right? Not when there are hundreds of apartments around with the lights off and no one even home! Is it such a crime? Home invasion or basic family survival instinct?

Final note. I don't plan to go light on you in this book. You will read and contemplate fresh common sense ideas and harsh realities. There are no "safe spaces" in cities where supermarkets have been empty for days, and you forgot to go to the store that week because you raced home to catch your favorite show.

I am compiling a real step by step plan here for you to pull your head out of your butt and survive. When its 3 am, the city has been dark for a week, and someone is trying every doorknob on your building floor. Morning sunshine!

I suppose you can give this book to your brother for Christmas and hope for the best right? I mean, it's not really going to happen or anything. Societies that were once thriving and fruitful don't actually devolve into lawless chaos, do they? Ask the citizens of Venezuela and Syria the same question.

You will be fine. Sleep tight now.

Chapter 1.

Mindset.

You will survive. Period. Not because you know all the angles. Not because you have every book and YouTube video memorized. Not because you can bench press your weight and do 20 pull ups…although that can't hurt. You will survive because you have the mindset to survive. Notice I am not telling you to get that mindset. I don't have to. You were born with it. You just let it go dormant as you worried about offending or insulting the fragile snowflakes you encounter every day.

You have always known the drug addicted bum on the corner could break a bottle over your head for a few bucks. You lock your doors and set your alarms without being told. You don't flash expensive watches and jewelry in an area that is, lets nicely, politely, say, populated by broke scum that will slit your throat for any of it.

You think about how you dress, where you park, what is happening around you and even check the location of exits when you get on a plane or attend a concert. You don't do this because you were taught it, you do it because you want to live! You have the mindset for survival right now. In you. Keep it at the ready because you will apply it in your daily life more deeply as you develop yourself into a prepared citizen.

The most important aspect of the survival mindset is to be decisive. Remember that? I told you I was proud of you for being decisive earlier. I am. Most people are lost to natural disasters because they did not prepare ahead of time or they did not act as the tornado was ripping town hall apart on its way to their home.

Just as a chess player can not know every possible scenario they will encounter in a match, you do not know every challenge you will be faced with in a survival situation. Preparation will help of course and even keeping yourself in shape is vital, but nothing can get you further than the will to survive.

The mindset that you will think about the dangers facing you decide the next move, and act. You will plan out and perform your next step because you have the mindset to survive. You are thirsty? Think, decide, act. You are cold? Think, decide, act. You are in danger? Think, decide, act.

When the documentary is made showing footage of the disaster you survived, I better see you with a backpack, expandable baton and a face of pure determination moving out towards your next destination. I better not see you huddled in a filthy mass of "sheeple," starring at the burning Red Cross tent and looking up to the sky, hoping for another helicopter to drop a few cases of canned dog food and concentrated milk.

Think, Decide, Act.

Chapter 2.

The rise of the City. A global look at urbanism and its effect on public safety.

Before metal and concrete skyscrapers were built to the clouds, communities were made to rely on themselves, not the constant flow of food and materials from the outside. The very idea of a town was that it had all its needs met from within its communal structure. Trade with outside villages allowed new and different goods to be acquired but was not an imperative. The community could always take care of itself.

In fact, walls were often built to hold off a siege from outside forces. Food and shelter contained inside with livestock and even agricultural production within. Good examples of this were seen in Europe before the rise of cities. A lord's land held a military force, food production, blacksmiths and homes for the population. Self reliant and secure.

How different the world lives today. The United Nations' research on human migration from rural areas into the city is shocking. In 2009 the UN estimated that 3 million people a week move into urban environments. In 2014 it was determined that the majority of the worlds population, 54%, lived in cities and that it could reach 66% by 2050.

Cities grow via three methods. First, immigration from the outside into the city. Second, the natural rise in the city's population itself and third, the reclassification of areas around the city, suburbs, as new urban districts. But why does this urban sprawl and mass migration occur?

Cities represent new opportunities to those who feel disenfranchised by their current situation. If a farmer loses the family business due to cheaper imported foods from outside the nation, the skills they have developed have little to no use. They move to the city in search of jobs and new industry. If war, natural disasters, floods, drought, and earthquakes, wreak havoc on smaller communities with no deep resources to recover and rebuild, the population seeks shelter and even future stability in the distant city. For them, the city, even in another country, means hope.

These situations have been seen in both North and South America as cultures move from farming and manufacturing to management and financial economies. What is the result of this migration out of the small village and into the big city? How does this change the citizens themselves? We now get to the root of the survival paradox.

The original idea of moving to the city may well have been for self preservation. A loss of job, home, a way of life created a need to make a change. What is quickly lost are the skills to build, grow, protect one's self, educate one's family. All these facets of life are expected to be provided by the shiny new world of the urban system. As the expectation of services grows, the ability to rely on yourself for basic needs drops. Not just the desire to take care of yourself, the ability to.

Cell phones and public services lower our self responsibility. We foolishly believe that help is a just a call away or that food is just around the corner. The sink backs up? Call a plumber. The car breaks down? Call a tow truck. We carry cards in our wallets and purses that make new clothes and hot food just a swipe away. We feel the security in fire stations, public transportation, ambulances and emergency rooms.

I ask you to look at the western world's shining cities when faced with peril. In New Orleans, after hurricane Katrina, the real shock was not that the city was flooded. That was expected. The fact that homes were half under water no power, supermarkets, and infrastructure destroyed, all these results were discussed by city planners and the local news media for years.

The real shock, the jaw dropper that left all Americans stunned and the remaining population of New Orleans facing death as a reality, was that services and responses planned and practiced by local and federal agencies were when tested, a joke. It was the images of citizens sleeping on their roofs, huddled in stadiums with no power or sanitation, or wandering the streets waste deep in sewer water looking for their next meal.

It was the wake up call that when a city, in all its glory and power, is hit with a real test to its emergency response capability, it collapses … fast. When a dense urban environment has its resources and resilience to recover from disaster tested by harsh circumstances and events, it fails miserably. It turns out that the strength of the city, its tightly packed, diverse population is as fragile as a fiberglass sailboat on a stormy sea.

The Western world watched and realized it could be any one of us in the same situation. From New York to Los Angeles, no matter what the size, no matter how much has been invested in its infrastructure, when it comes down to survival after a major terror strike or natural disaster… the only entity you can rely on is yourself.

Presented to you here is a no holds barred look at the three stages of self preservation after your city has lost its ability to secure your safety and freedoms. First, we will discuss the basic idea of awareness. This will contain the daily steps you can take to be prepared for situations as they arise. In this section, we will include the first few weeks of individual and family survival planning.

Second, the reality that you may very well need to move out of your location and traverse a lawless and dangerous cityscape to survive. The third and final stage represents society's inability to recover. At this point, your safety and basic freedoms are either not protected by or threatened by the very government you live under. Your only option, expatriation.

I told you I wouldn't go easy in this book. If you want rainbows and the gentle assurance that when your power goes off and isn't coming back on, the trucks are on the way with blankets and hot soup, I can't help you. Not because I want to scare you, far from it. I want you to understand, those trucks are not on the way. The courts, police, ACLU and every other house of cards that shelter our urban population of special snowflakes will be gone.

Its 4 am on a Thursday, the storm just got worse, your apartment's window just broke inward with torrential rain horizontally filling the living room. You scramble from the bed and reach for the light switch…click…nothing. Good morning.

Chapter 3.

Awareness.

Before an actual situation occurs in your city, I want you to live your life in a state of awareness. This means preparing for what could and most likely will, happen in your life that would lead to you being in a state of danger. First, we will look what scenarios threaten the safety of urban communities. Second, we will discuss the ways to protect yourself, your family, in the initial onset of a situation through the first 30 days of survival.

Natural disaster.

There is nothing new about hurricanes ravaging the coastal states or the earthquakes of Central America, California and the Mediterranean. Long before modern society existed these natural disasters have pounded local communities all over the planet.

The difference today is that the impact realized from these natural occurrences are more profound than ever. Primarily, this is due to a society that is reliant on supply lines originating far from its location.

Earthquakes that originate in the sparsely populated Yellowstone National Park are every bit as strong as those arising within San Francisco's city limits. The impact, however, is vastly different. Millions of lives are affected in California by powerful earthquakes. Roads and bridges are ruined. Power is lost and communications lines, including cell towers, are overburdened and ultimately useless.

Let's look at hurricane Iniki that made landfall directly over the Hawaiian island of Kauai in 1992. It was easy to explain how an isolated community, even with a low population density, could be crushed by a major storm. Of course, the supply chain is needed for food and medical supplies. How does this justify San Francisco's state of emergency following the earthquake of 1989? San Francisco is on the mainland of North America.

This again is asked about a simple road closure in Atlanta, Georgia in 2017. A sinkhole damaged highway brought the commerce and transportation of a major city to a standstill. The long term planning of major cities has not been thought through. I look at it as a "let's just see what happens" attitude. Well, lets not. Plan and prepare because ultimately your city government is not.

Terrorist attack.

I use the scenario of a dirty bomb, smuggled into the US via the Mexican border, in this book from time to time because it represents an attack that would bring all emergency services and infrastructure, city-wide, to a stop. Water, possibly contaminated, would be shut off. Emergency services of any kind would be unavailable as they are called in to deal with the decontamination and evacuation of citizens.

A dirty bomb is the least likely to ruin your day, or life, in the long list of terror attacks being carried out in the world's cities today. Hijacked trucks driven into busy walkways or lone wolf attacks using knives, firearms or small, homemade bombs are a weekly occurrence. You will be affected by one of these in your lifetime. The immediacy of this threat is the reason I wrote the first of the three stages of urban prep, Awareness.

The reasoning or ideologies behind terror attacks are deeply seated in disenfranchised communities around the world. Some want political change, other seek glory from their god. You can study and discuss these points on your own, I am only here to help save your ass from the outcome, a violent attack on a city's population for media coverage.

The collapse of the rule of law. Riot.

Watching video footage of the Los Angeles riots in 1992 was a wake up call for most Americans. A major city, in the United States, brought to its knees by a mass of humanity hell bent on destruction. Buildings were burned to the ground, shops looted and smashed, even drivers pulled from their vehicles and beaten with bricks and pipes.

Store owners took to their rooftops with assault rifles and armored vests. Citizens fled far from their workplaces and homes to find safety. Even to this day, Los Angeles bears the scars of this chaos and destruction. The lives of those affected would never be the same.

Taking a closer look at the city and state government reaction, it can be said that a major effort was made to contain and disrupt these violent actions using the police and even the National Guard. It was the time needed to mobilize and the slow movement forward to end the riots that were most evident to me. An effort was made, yes, but for hours and even days, the citizens of Los Angeles found themselves trapped in a city that was burning itself to rubble.

In 2017 we are again watching a new wave of civil unrest. Political and social-economic differences have led to violence in the streets and schools of major cities. European nations, Sweden, Asia, and even America, face daily demonstrations, car burnings, and physical violence. There is no time I can think of where major cities faced such a challenge of civic unrest and political divide all around the globe than today.

Words are the most feared weapon in our society. The force used to silence opposition will only get worse as we see the city, state, and national governments take sides in the melee, choosing when and if they are going to intervene. Again, you will have to protect yourself and family first.

A cyber attack on local, national infrastructure.

Spend one day keeping track of every aspect where electricity and internet connectivity plays a role in your life. Think through this critically. Electricity makes your building's elevators run, alarms and cameras function. Without it the trains and street traffic stop. Airports close. Supermarkets, gas stations, and convenience stores are locked for the day. Cell phone towers slowly drain their back up batteries over a few hours, then shut down.

Our financial networks are attacked by cyber threats 24 hours a day looking to exploit a weakness that could drain or reroute our accounts. Hackers or even foreign security agencies infiltrate government and major corporate networks. The intent is to gain secret information that could create vulnerabilities in our national security. We need to go much further than just signing up for identity theft protection and changing our passwords.

As I shift into the actions you can take to protect yourself from threats as they occur and extending into the first 30 days that you may be forced to survive, let me stay on the subject of cybersecurity. We will discuss how you can protect you and your family's privacy and money.

Identity theft.

We begin this section on how to protect yourself from the threat that happens behind your back, even while you sleep. Identity theft and cyber threats. More than 13 million adults in the United States were victims of identity fraud in 2015, according to federal law enforcement statistics. Over $15 billion in personal accounts were affected. Identity theft can take many forms, but one type of fraud occurs when an unauthorized credit account is opened.

A pair of major tools, fraud alerts, and security freezes, can help consumers fight back against such an action.

Fraud alert: Ask one of the three credit reporting companies to put a fraud alert on your credit report. It requires potential creditors to verify your identity before any new credit is issued in your name. A fraud alert lasts 90 days, and you can renew it.

Security freeze (Credit freeze): Ask one of the three credit reporting companies to put a security freeze on your credit report. This keeps potential creditors from seeing a credit report at all. No one can open a new line of credit in your name until the freeze is lifted.

Another valuable resource for the protection of your online identity is monitoring. Monitoring services are available from private companies that watch your personal information 24 hours a day. These services alert you if they believe your data is being used maliciously.

Credit monitoring tracks activity on your credit reports. You are alerted if a company checks your credit history, a new loan or credit card account is opened in your name, a creditor or debt collector says your payment is late, public records show that you've filed for bankruptcy, there is a legal judgment against you, your credit limits change, your personal information, like your name, address, or phone number, changes.

Identity monitoring alerts you when your personal information, like your bank account information or Social Security number, driver's license, passport, or medical ID number, is being accessed or shows up on change of address requests, court or arrest records, orders for new utility, cable, or wireless services, payday loan applications, check cashing offers, social media or websites that identity thieves use to trade stolen information.

Paperwork in order?

Another important step in your everyday readiness is to have your important documents in order. Recovering from a threat, whether it presents itself via the internet or in the physical world, means protecting your identity, what you own and what you have accomplished. Having important documents duplicated, dispersed and protected is a good plan.

A simple way of always having your passport, birth certificate and even deeds to property ready for presentation is to take quality scans or photos of these documents, email them to yourself and then store them in a folder on your email account. This allows fast recovery of these documents if lost. Emails from insurance companies, online vehicle registration proofs, vocational certifications, and degrees should be moved to this folder as well.

Save your documents onto a CD or USB drive and have your parents lock it in their home safe. After a fire, flood or flight from your property, you may not have access back to recover deeds, insurance proofs, birth certificates or veteran status paperwork. The idea is to reduce the recovery time of these documents. Government services will be overburdened with requests from unprepared citizens.

I make a copy of precious photos on to a USB drive about every year and give them to my parents as a gift. They keep the drives locked up, protecting these irreplaceable memories.
Cloud storage drives are great if you can maintain them. The problem is we forget to, and when they reach max capacity, photos are no longer uploaded.

An observation needs to be made about the safety and reliability of online sites. Keep social media for just that, social and casual conversations. Do not discuss personal, financial or political information. Stay upbeat and polite. Social media is often a weak point in your identity protection. Never store or display personal information, addresses, phone numbers, email accounts on social media. Work numbers and emails are useful for business purposes, of course.

More people are reducing their online media footprint. I think this will be a useful and wise trend in the future.

Phone numbers at the ready.

Start and keep updated a document containing all your most valuable financial, medical plan numbers. Have the customer service numbers and card numbers for each of your credit cards. Medical insurance numbers for you and your family members. Social security numbers, allergies, blood types. Bank accounts, vehicle, and home insurance account numbers.
This is a one stop shop to open when you need this info.

Back up this document to the cloud and email it to yourself. Keep it on your cell phone. As long as its readily accessible, but password protected.

How to pack and store for survival.

So far we have gone over some basic scenarios and thoughts on everyday awareness to be safe and prepared in the urban environment, lets shift gears into what you will need, physically.

Everyday items in your backpack.

Carry these items in a separate pocket or just inside your daily use backpack in case you find yourself at work or in transit between work and your home when a dangerous scenario begins:

Flashlight, with a headband, is best. You could find yourself on public transportation, subway or train when city power is lost. In this common scenario, things will go dark and don't rely on the emergency lighting systems that most bankrupt cities cannot maintain.

Water. In a crushproof bottle, fill it each morning and toss it in your bag.

Protein bars. Stress and physical activity will burn calories. You daily wear backpack should have a few meal replacement bars in it. There will be no restaurants or convenience stores to get food as you try to get home.

Communication. Have your cell as well as charging cables, extra USB rechargeable power brick, and headphones. Initially cell towers are overwhelmed, but eventually, you will get text messages through to family and friends as you make your way home or to another safe location.

Medications and first aid kit. If you need prescription medications, have a few days worth in a bottle in your bag. Prepare a small first aid kit with gauze, wrap bandages and sunblock. Sprained ankles, deep cuts, and long walks outdoors are all real possibilities as you make way to get home.

Cash. There are no ATMs, banks or credit card machines if the city power goes out.

Duct tape (just a few yards wrapped around your medications bottle) whistle, safety pins and hard candy for the sugars/energy.

Water filter survival pen. Google this and pick a few up on eBay. You can drink water out of a muddy pond or concrete gutters.

Knife and multitool. These will always be useful to you, and the blade should be where you can get to it fast for self protection. For added security, have a short metal pipe in the back of your desk drawer at work. You will carry this as you trek home in case of an emergency where public transit is unavailable, but no need to carry on you daily.

How to stage your vehicle.

Prepping your vehicle for a survival situation is very important. In a city, you may have to shelter in your car for days. Blizzards, terror attacks that shut down highways and earthquakes that take out bridges will leave you stuck in your car until you make your next plan or until public services are restored. Here are some items to keep in a bag in your car:

Everything from your daily backpack prep: Water, protein bars, cell phone extra power brick, protein bars, medications, cash, knife, and multitool.

Larger and better stocked first aid kit including burn gels and wraps.

Another water filter survival pen and a crushable, plastic water carry bag.

Flashlight and batteries. Preferably one that has LED lamp lights to light up the interior of your vehicle, as well as a power forward, directed beam.

Wool blankets and reflective material "space" blanket. If you live in an area prone to major snow or foul weather conditions you may already have these in your car. If you live in a warmer area, you may have to travel to a colder climate in an emergency, so pack at least one wool and one reflective material blanket.

Gas siphon to remove gas from another vehicle if need be.

Gas can. I talk about having 5 gallons of gas stored in your home or garage safely in the "hunker down" section. If it can be safely stored, it's a good idea.

Escape tool, window smasher, and seat belt cutter combo.

Shovel for clearing mud and snow if you get stuck.

Fire extinguisher.

Extra oil and coolant.

Spare tire and jack. Check these from time to time to make sure the tire is inflated, and you know how to use the jack.

Solar charger for the battery. These are available on eBay pretty cheap.

Small transistor radio with batteries and a headphone jack to stay informed.

Toilet paper.

Emergency shelter, tent. This can be small and easy to stuff in a backpack.

Gas masks for each family member. Good gas masks can be found online for around forty dollars.

Hiking shoes and a spare set of outdoor clothing.

12 volt to 120 volt inverter. This will allow you to run electrical items off your car battery if need be. Not too expensive and good to have in your kit.

Fold up bike. This is a good item for when your vehicle will no longer get you out. Clogged roadways or running out of gas can lead to abandoning your vehicle and heading out on bike. This may seem like overkill, but you can enjoy the bike anytime and keep it stored in your car.

Camouflage tarp to throw over your vehicle with tie down cords.

Misc. items: Jumper cables, bungee cords, a roll of duct tape, rope, toolkit and electrical repair kit, gloves.

Preparing your home for the first 30 days of survival.
"Hunker down" mode.

Now that we have gone over the basic items you should have on hand for daily life and travel in the city, let's move on to staging a good prep kit in your home. Keep your items together in that lower back cabinet you hate trying to get into. Except for the firearm, which should be locked in a quick unlock case under your bed.

Everything from your daily backpack prep: Water, protein bars, cell phone extra power brick, protein bars, medications, cash, knife, and multitool. Just keep them in your daily backpack, at the ready, to flee the house if need be.

Water. For each person expected to be in the apartment or house, I would keep a case of bottled water or even two.

Water filter survival pens for each family member. These are not expensive or large. I travel with one when outside the United States. They are about $15 each and can be very valuable as a form of currency for trading when cash is no longer accepted.

Water carry bags. You may have to venture out and get unfiltered fresh water from any nearby source, return to your home and filter it.

Water Desalination. If you live near the ocean, a desalination device may be expensive upfront but can result in an unlimited water supply for your family.

Food. I don't suggest spending a fortune on fancy survival foods, but if you want to go ahead. A cheaper way is to pick up 30 cans of pork and beans or canned beef stew per person. You will get protein and carbs. In many cases, you can find these on sale for less than a dollar a can.

Protein bars. These are easy to use as currency to get supplies from neighbors.

Coffee. You will want it, and if it's in single serve dehydrated form, it will work as currency as well.

First aid kit with advanced items for burns, broken bones (splint kit) and eye injuries. You can assemble the items yourself online rather cheap as opposed to buying a major kit. I will include a good home first aid kit checklist in the checklist section of the book.

First aid and other family/emergency medical information books.

30 day supply of hygiene products, toilet paper. Baby wipes are good for an alternate shower plan.

30 days of pet supplies if need be.

30 day supply of prescription medications. A full antibiotic prescription as well. Pain medications, prescription strength the best. This will help you cope with the pain of an injury so you can focus and think.

Fire extinguisher.

Multivitamins, chewable.

Flashlights, LED lamps and batteries. A solar battery charger is a nice to have, but battery supplies are fine for 30 day survival situations.

Battery operated or hand crank rechargeable radio. AM/FM/SW radios are not expensive and will keep you informed when the power goes out. A transistor radio and batteries with a headphone jack is must have for your kit.

Cell phone and all chargers, power bricks.

Personal/portable power pack with inverter and outlets. These remain plugged in until needed. They can give you one or two home outlets for several hours if required. These often come with a 12 volt, 120 volt and USB outlet. They may even have auto battery jumping capability.

All important documents in a waterproof container to be packed in a backpack fast. Deed, medical insurance proofs, birth certificates, social security cards, globally accepted certifications for work skills, college degrees, a few photos of family members show others if searching for them.

Duct tape, bungee cords, heavy trash bags, several 1'X2" boards to repair windows.

Sewing kit.

A handgun in locking, quick access, case under the bed with a powerful flashlight inside it as well. Practice opening the case in the dark.
Extra ammunition.
The second handgun sealed in a waterproof bag and sewn/ zipped inside of furniture fabric.   This is not proper storage for a loaded firearm but will give you a back up if law enforcement begins to collect weapons. This handgun can be listed as lost while in transit to a local shooting range in an official police case to keep it off firearm collection lists.

Long gun, rifle, shotgun. These weapons will offer more power and accuracy at longer ranges, but most important, they will scare away dangerous people. The sound of a shotgun being hand loaded/operated behind a front door will often keep it from being kicked in.

All firearm repair and cleaning supplies, documentation, and holsters.

Less than lethal protection. Pepper spray is not an effective indoor weapon but can be used if you venture out to get water and supplies. Expandable batons are great, but you need to learn to use them or else they can be taken away and used against you.

Booby traps. A cord that can be placed across the floor about ankle height, even more than one, will trip home invaders that forcefully enter. This gives you time to beat them or shoot them, which you should.

Whistles, air horns. These can alert other people or emergency services if they are in the area and you need them.

Bright orange plastic tarp. This can be the back of a reflective survival blanket. Use this to alert helicopters to your location if you fled to the roof of your building. A strobe light can be useful at night for this.

Writing supplies and notebook.

Items to secure the door. Shims for under the door, wood, nails, hammer. You will need this if your door is kicked in damaging the lock set. Using one lock and saving the deadbolt as a second lock device is an option. Chains and sliding deadbolts are easy to add to the door as backups.

Warm blankets, towels and other supplies you may need if there are no washing machine services for 30 days, which they won't be.

Vodka. I know this sounds odd, but in many parts of the world, grain alcohol is used as easily transferable currency. In Russia, its swapped for gasoline as common as cash. Stock several 750ml bottles of the lowest grade vodka you can find. It won't go bad, and no one will care what brand it is.

Gas. If you can safely store 5 gallons of gas in your home, it is a good idea. There will not be gas stations available, and it may give you mobility until these services return.

Gold. The value of gold at the time of writing this book hovers around $1200 an ounce. In a situation where your local and national and economy is hit hard by a major disaster or terrorist attack, you may have to rebuild your wealth. A fall in the value of the national currency to ten percent of its current value would destroy the savings of most citizens. You need to be ready for this, not frightened, but ready. I suggest at least $10000 in gold coin secured in a safe in your home. Another $10000 at least in the safe deposit box of a bank in another state. Perhaps where you have a family, but I don't want o get ahead of myself here.

A plan for your family.

Now that we have gone over the prepping of your home, vehicle and person for situations that could occur at any time and without warning, we need to discuss family. If you are a hermit whose only loved ones are an AR-15, a case of good whiskey and an Asian, life size silicon love doll, well…besides being totally awesome, …you can skip this section.

It's not easy to talk to "non-preppers" about society collapsing or tornadoes tearing through major urban cityscapes, but there is a way to breach the subject. Find a recent article online about a disaster or terror attack. Text the article to your family and add "are we ready for something like this?"

Another way is to bring up a recent incident when you are driving with them. I like to ask them what they would do, get them thinking. This often leads to your family members asking what you would do. Be ready with a quick line. Something like, "hey, I'm ready, I have all sorts of stuff stashed in the kitchen right now for us. Just remember, get home, ok?"

This gets us to an important idea, your family needs to know where to go if something happens. If its possible to move in the city, they may be able to get home. If they have to flee the city, they could end up miles from you. They need a communication plan if that happens. Text a group text ring to everyone. Use it now and then to send a funny photo or Meme. The idea is that if anything happens, one contact attempt will notify all of where they are.

Your family needs a place to meet. If the home you live in cannot be reached, where will you meet? Do not go to the most commonly chosen location in town, it will be packed with thousands of people trying to find loved ones. It might be a start, but finalize a site about a block away from it.

Have a secondary location as well and finally an area outside the city if you each need to flee separately. Your kids may have to go on a bus provided by the school. You may end up on foot heading another direction. An email may be best if phones are not available, make sure yours is simple to remember.

To give an example, here in Hawaii, where I am writing this book, we plan for tsunamis as hurricanes for the most part. If there is a possible tsunami or an inbound storm, we have a strong home to go to where all the family will meet. It is high enough to escape the storm surge, a high inland heading surge of water that comes with a hurricane. It is also in a protected building with supplies. The family knows that is the location. Get there.

If you live on the mainland, you have a significant advantage over us in Hawaii. We are foolishly packing a million people on a tiny island with little to no food production. You can move to another state if need be. This should be in your plans and make sure your family chooses a relative's home to go to. You can relocate later, but as a backup, outside your city, make sure everyone knows what town to go to.

Schools have emergency plans in place so your children could be in a better situation than you and your spouse. If roads are closed or so packed with traffic that people abandon their vehicles, you will have to go on foot to get your kids. They will have food, water, and shelter at the school. Make sure you have what you need to get them home. If need be, get supplies from home first, then to the school. A rash emotional decision will leave you and your kids walking the streets at midnight without defense.

Chapter 4.

Social commentary: A woman's place in the (post-apocalyptic) world.

According to the Census Bureau, 35 million households in America are occupied by a lone dweller. A person living alone. In fact, in the urban environment, single occupant dwellings exist as high as 40 percent in major cities as of 2010. This has placed millions of women in apartments and condos alone. Not even a roommate.

How does this affect the reality of survival for these women when there is no more power, water supply and law enforcement in a chaotic densely populated city? The possibility of rape, murder, assault, robbery, burglary and home invasion will be higher than ever, with no emergency services available. No communication to call for them if they were available. Let's consider this carefully.

Sexual Dimorphism.

Sexual dimorphism is the physiological reality that women are not as strong, fast or prone to brute force if placed in a dangerous situation, as a man is. It is a scientific reality that the prepper female must overcome. I understand just hearing these ideas now can make the female readers angry, this is a symptom of a much larger problem.

As a society we have been lying to women, promising a knight in shining blue uniform to come running if anyone even touches them wrong. A false sense of security will place millions of American women in a precarious, deadly position when there are no police, building security or women's rights groups to come running when the front door is kicked in.

Be honest with yourself, ladies, you need a gun. Period. You need an intermediate weapon like a stun gun for indoors and a can of mace for outdoors, sure, but ultimately, you need a handgun. You cant buy it, you have to go to a state safety course and tack on a basic handling course for good measure. Self confidence, a strong body, and a sharp mind will get you far in a post-societal-collapse world, but a gun will keep you alive.

Team up.

There are other women you know in your building. You have talked to them at the pool, elevator or laundry room. Get to know a name or two. Have them over for a glass of wine to make them comfortable with you. You may need them to stay alive if the police or security in your building can't help you. Together, two or three women can repel far more brute force coming at them than one.

Find a man. In your building, perhaps a friend or co-worker, family member or otherwise, plan to have a man in league with you when faced with a survival situation. Maybe more than one. This goes back to the idea of making a team, making you a stronger force.

Do your friends have a plan? If not, tell them to get to your place in case of an emergency. They can stay with you if things come to a full stop in your city and don't look like they are coming back for a few days or weeks. Don't be dramatic, just let them know, they will remember.

Plan for these situations by having an extra case of water, canned food and perhaps a second gun for them. Lets even suggest here, that you train with your handgun at the range about once every few months, inviting a friend to go with you "just for fun." She will love it, of course, but you will have a more prepared fighting partner when you need her.

Sexual dimorphism is a biological reality. The effect of a .38 caliber round hitting an intruder in the chest is also a biological reality. These two realities are yours to choose from, now, before it is too late to prepare for them. I will include a section of links at the end of the book to find out how to get licensed and trained to use a firearm properly in your state. Oh…and the pink rubberized handles for your Smith and Wesson .357 magnum…love it!

Chapter 5.

Leaving your home, moving to another location.
"Bug out" mode.

Let's consider that any of the proposed scenarios has occurred and lasted longer than two weeks or even 30 days. You may very well need to move out of your city and relocate to a safer area. Mobility in a lawless town will be a dangerous option, but the reality is you may very well have to move to survive.

In the military, we were taught to act strangely in foreign nations when confronted with danger. Walk with a limp, talk to yourself. We have shone videos of persons using these techniques and being left alone in dangerous confrontations. Avoid conversations. Don't make eye contact. Move slowly through crowds and don't attract attention. When you are past those areas, move out faster and make up for time.

Let's look at mobility in a fractured urban environment.

First, why are you leaving? What has made you leave your apartment? Are you out of food, water, other supplies? Have you been attacked and can no longer defend yourself and your family at your present location? Is there a growing threat that you want to stay ahead of?

All of these are reasonable scenarios. Any of them could mean packing your "bug out" bag and moving to a new location. What are you bringing? Where are you going? Let's take these step by step.

Moving from your apartment means that you are either out of supplies or in danger beyond what you can protect yourself from in your home. The items you carry will be light and practical. Things to keep you alive and defend yourself. Here are some examples of your "bug out" kit and planning your exit:

A weathered bag that will blend with the city. No $200.00 North Face yellow climber's specials! Stay humble and quiet. Do not attract attention to yourself with fancy items.

Defensive weapon. I like a short metal pipe myself. Let's consider this, it will never run out of ammo, you can move fast with it, it does not attract attention, and it can be hidden easily. A short pipe will also swing quickly opposed to the long arc of a baseball bat that can be taken from you and used against you.

Offensive weapon. A handgun, period. I love the idea of a rifle for power and to keep threats at a distance, but there is little chance moving through a lawless city with one. You will have to blast your way through, wasting ammo, eventually dumping it. If you have a short AR-15, you could hide it and have a handgun at the ready for unexpected encounters. Perhaps this is the best combination.

Have you trained with a handgun? Your town will have indoor ranges that offer weekend courses in handgun safety. Sign up, take them. When you choose your weapon, consider your skills. If you feel you can clear a weapon that has a problem and won't fire, invest in a good semi automatic pistol and several magazines. If your skills are beginner level and you have only taken the state safety courses for ownership, buy a revolver. If it fails to fire, just pull the trigger again!

First aid kit. Like always, I am not talking about a "boo boo kit" designed for cuts and scrapes. You need the gauze, tape and wraps to secure a serious injury and keep moving forward. Soldiers learn to carry such items in a pocket, so they do not have to dig through their bags for them. Have anti-bacterial gel and other basic things for when you find shelter, but keep major items in a pants side pocket ready to grab. I have included a first aid section in this book for you to read over. Don't be afraid to take your local Red Cross Advanced First Aid or CPR courses. They are excellent. Take them with your family.

Easy food and water supplies. Based on your time to destination, plan your food and water needs. Keep it light and bring what you need to survive, no extras unless you have candy that won't melt. Candy can be used as currency to get other things. So can lightweight items like anti-bacterial gels and dehydrated coffee packets. All light and valuable.

Destination plans. Where the hell are you going? If you need to move out of the city, decide where you want to be at the end of each day. By dark, be at that destination and hold there. Have your route planned and ultimately where you want to go. If the way is blocked, have your alternate routes figured out as well.

New home. I recommend an alternate place to live inside the US and ultimately, outside. I will discuss expatriation in detail later, but for this time consider another town or state to move on to. Have bank accounts prepared for when you arrive? National banks are best. Look into this new home, the culture, visit it.

I have always loved the idea of cold and miserable areas to escape to. I believe most people, in a survival situation, will go South. Searching for warmth. I plan to go North. Cold, High altitude and remote.

Clothing. Your clothing should allow you to move without gathering attention. No fancy or loud clothes, bags, shoes, electronics, weapons or any other valuable gear. Keep it under a baggy hooded sweatshirt or jacket. Look cheap, filthy and uninteresting. Have a pair of sturdy hiking shoes, rain gear, warm or sun blocking hat, cargo shorts, and other comfortable, durable clothing ready in your "bug out" kit.

Shelter. A small tent is good but can attract attention. A plastic tarp over you can be better. It looks…unprepared. Like you grabbed what you could, and that's it.

Money, documents, and ID. Take only what you need and remember that if you have second copies at your family's house, emailed to you, do not burden yourself with every last document you have. Paper gets heavy! ID, passport, the most important documents. Put them in a waterproof ziplock bag, stuff them and get moving.

Gold already in a safe deposit box in the state you have decided to "bug out" to in case of an emergency situation. Probably a state you have visited often and know well. Does family live there? Did you work there before and know the environment? Start a bank account there and keep a few thousand in a savings account as well as the gold in the safe deposit box.

Form a team.

If you have to bug out, why go alone? I understand that most millennials are now living alone, but when you head to your next destination, in an emergency situation, why not bring a team? We are often looking at survival as a lone wolf scenario. The reality is that you may have neighbors, friends or family members that will travel with you. This can provide security.

Casually discuss these ideas with friends. Let them know that if something were to happen, they could move on with you. A group of 5 will not be messed with like a couple or an individual might.

Uncomfortable realities.

Fighting to survive.

I explained earlier that you want to blend and not attract attention when moving in a dangerous urban environment. Never make eye contact and don't be distracted. Trouble, however, will find you and when it does, hit it hard.

Never allow yourself to be pulled into a verbal or physical confrontation move around it. If that becomes unavoidable, this is where a short steel pipe can be much more effective than a gun. A gunshot means you have resources. A pipe means you don't or at least they are limited. Keep the gun at the ready but swing low and hard with that pipe.

Take the legs out before you arch back and go for the head. Head strikes are expected. Keep your eyes around waist level and look around you. When you fight, fight to survive, hit hard and fast and then move. Never stay to fight longer.

Shooting to kill.

If you are surrounded by multiple attackers or confronted with someone who has a superior weapon to yours, you will have to use your firearm. Keep the firearm relatively low and pulled back to your body, don't extend your arm or point it at one of the group. This exposed you to have it taken away.

Point the barrel outward and down at a 45-degree angle, pull it back to you, move on and don't stop. If one of these attackers makes a forward move towards you, push the weapon out with both hands, fire at the center mass of their body, pull back fast and move on. Don't stop moving.

If someone gets to close and you can't fire for any reason, keep the weapon close to your body with your strong hand and use the other hand to shove them hard, preventing them from getting a hold of you. The reality is you may have to shoot more than one of them to survive, do it.

Dealing with the dead.

As you move, you may encounter a gruesome reality, the dead. From the natural disaster, the terrorist attack or from the lawless society that followed it, this is a real possibility. Do not go near or disturb a body at rest on the ground. It is easily a trap waiting for a "good Samaritan" to investigate. Go around, keep moving.

As a kid, my father was a US Marine and stationed in Detroit Michigan. It was not uncommon to drive through the city and see a body in the street. The protocol was just to keep driving. Trap or not, do not stop.

There is also the possibility that you will lose a member of your team as dangerous elements on your journey test you. The result of a fall or violence. If you care about them, do not give up, do not stop moving. If there are personal items on them that need to get to their family, this should be made clear before you, and your team move out.

Moving the wounded.

Another reality is that you or a team member may get wounded. I am going to include an emergency first aid section for you to read and become for familiar with. As I stated earlier, take a Red Cross Advanced First Aid course in your area.

If you have to move a wounded team member, it is fastest to get transportation. Bribes and a promise to join in your journey will work best if you do not have a vehicle. Otherwise, taking turns carrying this person may not be a reality if you or they have not maintained your health over the years. If you are weak or they are fat, you are fucked. Try to think about this now and make some changes in your life.

Moving the wounded can also exacerbate an injury. This person may have held up at a shelter, established by emergency services or created by you from what you can find. If no shelter can be found, they will have to make a hard choice. Move on and possibly open a wound further, or stay and wait for emergency services.

Chapter 6.

Social Commentary: A case for the light and mobile citizen.

The next big job, the next opportunity, will most likely not be in your city. It will be in another city, in another state or even another country. This is the highly connected and mobile world we live in. I want to prove this to you. Try this experiment.

Google your job, the best opportunity in your field whatever it may be. Use the keywords experience and relocation as well. What did you find? I would imagine you found that in, let's say, Jakarta, you found an open position that pays twice what you are making right now. Well, wasn't that fun?

Why can't you take that position? What is holding you back? I will tell you, you are anchored down. Like many in the workforce today, especially above the age of 30, you are tied by debt and foolish obligations to where you live. You have committed to a city that has not given you everything you gave to it.

The millennials and generation Z know that the next job will not be three blocks from your current job. In fact, you will be lucky if it's in the same city. Big corporations and exciting new startups do not care where you are, they care what you know. They expect you to have experience and to show up next week Monday, ready to work.

It is a fool's errand to tie yourself to a particular location in this day and age. There is a case to be made for the light and mobile citizen. Renting over owning a condo or home, using public or shared transportation, maintaining certifications that can be globally accepted. This is stability and mobility at the same time. This is the world we live in today.

Your professional training and higher education needs to be accepted in any state, or nation on earth. A teaching certificate or a nursing degree that is only acceptable in a particular state will immobilize you and hinder your opportunities.

Technology certifications are now accepted globally. Education and experience in engineering, life sciences, and medicine are as well. Take a serious look at where you are in your career. Could you move to that next amazing opportunity? If the answer is no, you need to fix that.

Let's go beyond your globally accepted, or not, vocational certifications. Are you anchored down by debt, memberships to local gyms with no national or global presence, long-term leases, and mortgages? If you can rent your condo in 30 days and fly to the United Arab Emirates for the 200k plus a year job, ill give you a pass. Most likely, you have signed on to a long term lease to save money, a mortgage that's upside down and a "sweetheart" at home who you couldn't make it without.

Ask yourself a simple question, what if it were the 1990s and you lived in Detroit, owned a home with a 30 year mortgage and your only job experience was mounting doors on a Cadillac? You would be homeless today. Many of those door mounters are just that.

Before you get yourself too deep in the quagmire, break those chains. Today, any working man or woman needs to be highly mobile. When the next opportunity knocks, even thousands of miles away, you should at least have the option to go. Ask the 20 year steel mill workers in Pittsburg if they want their kids to study the steel foundry sciences or become globally certified airline pilots. Ask the Bourbon street bartenders who lived through hurricane Katrina if they want their kids to sling drinks or program web applications.

Your life and livelihood may very well hang on whether you can pick up and leave, fast. Changes happen quickly today. Companies fold in one month. Think longtime Enron employees who drove to work in 2001, after working at the company for a decade, and found the doors chained. Did they have degrees and certifications that would be accepted in another state? Where are they sitting on a mortgage and house full of furniture bought on equity loans?

Survival means mobility in many cases. I'm not just talking in natural disasters. I'm talking in corporate and economic disasters. Build a life that transferable, transportable and uproot able in a pinch. Remember my recommendations about having a bank account in another state at the ready? When you get there, you should have an idea of the employment opportunities and what certifications they will expect you to have. Keep them up to date. Others will be moving too, stay in front of the crowd.

Financial stability can protect you from swings in the economy, lost opportunities at work or any other need to stop working, move and retrain. A good way to protect yourself is with multiple streams of income. This is not as hard as you think and you can start this year. Let's look at some ideas.

What is your retirement invested in? Most likely well diversified mutual funds and overall that is smart. I would ask you to consider dividend paying stocks such as telecom and utilities as well. Companies like Verizon and AT&T pay good annual dividends that can be either folded into your stock portfolio or pulled as income in a pinch.

Don't shortchange Asia-Pacific income funds either. Many of these pay 7% annually. Much of Southeast Asia is like the United States in the 1920s, a messy manufacturing powerhouse that is just moving upwards.

If you have bought an apartment or condo, could it be rented at a net gain if the need arose? Real estate investments in certain market areas can bring in a monthly income. Don't just think residential, a storage facility can be rented to a company or a local public agency for a long term lease. Commercial rentals can be excellent earners.

You may think real estate is risky, but what other investment can you live in if you had to? I would take a condo that rents well over sketchy municipal bonds any day. Google Puerto Rico bankruptcy as well as Detroit. As of 2015, 77 cities in California are on the economically challenged list. Your property is insured, if it burns to the ground, you get a check.

Finally, co-ownership in a local business or a second business that can move with you are good, stable backup money makers. Weekend work in photography, small business computer upgrades, network management or carpentry skills are ideas that can mean fast employment and cash in your pocket in an emergency relocation scenario.

Chapter 7.

Expatriation.

In the first section of this book, we discussed the everyday preparation for an emergency situation that could last a day for up to 30 days. We then went on to discuss the real possibility that you may have to "Bug out" and move out of your neighborhood, home, city altogether. In this section, we are going to discuss the third and most extreme measure you can take in a total societal collapse or oppressive government scenario, expatriation.

Expatriation is the decision to move yourself and your family out of your current country. Could this decision be made due to a natural disaster? Yes of course. We saw that in Chile after massive earthquakes left many sections of the country in ruins. With a bleak economic reality facing them and a country that was looking at years of reconstruction, many Chileans moved.
What about terrorism or war outbreak? This is quite common as we see today with the migration out of the middle east into Europe to escape War and terror.

The economic state of your country is not a factor. Look at the 2011 tsunami that hit Tohoku Japan, killing over 15,000 people and cracked the foundation of the Fukushima Nuclear Plant sending radioactive water and particles into the surrounding communities and groundwater. The economy of Japan was hit for certain, but it did not crumble. Japan's economy today, this book is being written five years later in 2017, is strong and vibrant. Many of the citizens who lived in Japan during the tsunami and radioactive fallout disasters decided to leave. They moved to the United States as well as other countries around the world. The reasoning was varied, but health concerns and a national media that was, and many believe still is, covering up the extent of the disaster left Japanese citizens skeptical of their government.

In the 17th century, a group of disaffected English citizens, the Puritans, left the safety and security of home to venture far across the sea. They deported to the new world, the colonies, which are now the United States of America.

In fact, in modern times we have seen the flight of Mexicans North find better work and a new life. We have seen Australian men move to Thailand, Bali and Vietnam in such numbers that as of 2016 Melbourne and Sydney have 30 percent less college educated men than women. The recent meltdown of the Venezuelan government has caused a mass migration out of the country. Some of Venezuela's citizens are choosing to no North to the United States and some to other South American nations.

Expatriation is not a new idea nor is it going to end anytime soon. The questions I pose to you in this chapter are:

What would be your deal breaker reason to leave your home country for good?
Do you have a plan for expatriation?
Have you put your plan in motion?

Let's look at scenarios that could cause you to say, "This is no longer working, I'm out."

Disarming of the population. The banning ownership and gathering of personal firearms is the first step to total government control of a population. Until then, there is always self-determination, self reliance, and self security factor. Without firearms, none of those exist. One's safety is decided upon by the government, or not if your political views run askew of the ruling party.

Economic opportunities are bleak. In the United States today it is not uncommon for adults to return to school to completely reinvent their careers. The fact that the US economy is strong and many industries are looking for hardworking hires makes retraining an option. With the rise of artificial intelligence, many jobs will be lost to automation. Drivers, teachers, human resources, administrators, finance and accounting jobs, the list keeps going. New opportunities may not balance unemployment.

No freedom of speech. The most overlooked, underappreciated and misunderstood freedom is the freedom of speech. Without it there would never have been the opening discussions of why slavery is wrong, women deserve equal rights, or that abortion should be legal. The political party would have crushed these ideas in power at the time, and those who discussed them would have been criminals! No new ideas can be brought forward without freedom of speech. Without it, a country is stuck, ceases to progress and begins a downward spiral. New ideas, especially those not popular, cannot be openly discussed and considered.

Government surveillance. The year this book was written, 2017, information was found by hackers and leaked to the world that the Central Intelligence Agency of the United States was not only performing advanced surveillance on people of interest around the world but of Americans as well. It was posted to a website called Wikileaks and admitted to by the agency. Furthermore, the online tools they were using were so powerful, they could turn hundreds of mobile electronic devices in any given area into cameras and microphones to used by the CIA for their surveillance without the knowledge or consent of the owners. With more and more advanced surveillance and monitoring facilities being built by the CIA and the National Security Agency (NSA), the very idea of privacy is waning.

Natural disaster. In the United States, if a tornado tears through your town, you can rebuild or, if anything, travel to a nearby state to start over again. In smaller countries, it is possible that a major hurricane or earthquake could permanently disable the nation. The system of law, emergency services and other facets of government may collapse.

Major terror attack/war causes societal collapse. For this, I am discussing the use of an EMP, electromagnetic pulse weapon, on the country you live in. An EMP weapon is detonated high in the atmosphere above a target city or country. The higher it is detonated, the wider spread the effects. EMP weapons emit a powerful electronic pulse that destroys any device that is operated by electronic circuitry, especially those that have transistors and circuit boards. Computers, cars, public transportation, hospital equipment, cell phones…everything stops. The chaos that ensues would cause you to go directly into "hunker down" mode in your home. Most likely over time, if the attack was widespread enough, you may have to expatriate out of your country.

What is your plan?

Sit down and think about where you would go, yourself and your family if need be, in the case that your current nation was no longer a viable option. I went over the various conditions that could make you move, but where? Have you been outside of your current nation? What do you know about different cultures, languages, currencies, conditions of life outside of your home?

My first suggestion to you is to travel. Plan a trip and go. Go light, enjoy yourself, no heavy luggage, just a good backpack you can carry on the plane, your cell, and laptop if you need them. Before you go, watch lots of videos from travelers to that country to learn dangers and tips. Prepare for your trip and have fun, but remember, it's a fact finding mission.

On your trip research and gather paperwork, brochures, etc. on the following subjects:

Immigration laws and citizenship.
Banks, bank accounts, safe deposit boxes, investments.
Credit card services
The job market, fields that pay and are in demand.
Hospitals and clinics. Is your insurance taken? Costs of service if in cash.
Dental clinics including costs in cash.

Cost of housing, apartments, and homes. Rental costs.
Legal help in your language, gather names and don't be afraid to walk in and shake a few hands.
Interact with the locals and figure out how much of the local language you would need to get by. If you lived there you would pick up much more, of course, but how much would you need to be effective and get integrated fast.
Networks of expats. Your country or another may have resources to help with integration and even moving.
If a restaurant owner or bartender is fluent in your language, make friends. Buy them a drink and have a conversation. Ask a few light questions about the culture and how expats fare, are accepted or not, can do better.
Travel options within the country. How are the bus and train services? Route brochures are often available.
Weather and natural dangers that should be known and accounted for if you live there.
Educational services if you have children that would need to relocate to a local school.
Crime rates. If you see a paper in your language at a café, read it. Check online also.
Firearm laws, gun ranges and other self defense laws. I have found that several countries, like the Philippines for example, are quite friendly to firearm ownership and use. It is not uncommon for locals to be well armed.

With this information, you have made a successful fact finding mission. Much of this you may be able to gather off the internet, sure, but to truly understand any culture you need to make several trips there and get familiar with it. The good and the bad, no country is perfect, but what we are looking for here are good options.

After you have explored at least two options and done good research in the points I mentioned above, you can make a plan to expatriate to one, perhaps prepare for either one. Here are some steps to take:

Immigration and citizenship laws should be discussed with a lawyer in that country. Book time, sit down and learn what you would need to show up with your family and not be deported. Under what conditions could you remain? In some countries, you need a financial investment to get permanent visa status.

Set up a bank account in the country including a safe deposit box. In the bank account put a few thousand dollars and make sure you will not be charged annually for nonuse. Small interest rates are fin for a savings account, you want it to remain open and not depleted over time.
In the safe deposit box you will need the following paperwork; A copy of all important documents, birth certificates, veteran documents, passports, land and home deeds, important certifications and degrees, proof of vocational training of any kind, important photos and photos of all loved ones. Anything you can think would be lost if you walked away right now and got on a plane, copy it, put it in the safe deposit box.

In the safe deposit box, you want at least $10000 worth of gold coin.   Shoot for above 10 ounces if possible. It may take you a few trips to get it there, I recommend traveling with about $2500 worth on each trip for a total of four trips. In the case that the united states dollar is no longer of value or falls considerably, the pure gold coin is a great way to reestablish yourself in a foreign country. At the time of writing this, gold trades at about $1200 an ounce. If the value of the US dollar were to fall and bottom out at 10 percent of its current state, each ounce of gold would be worth ten times the amount. In a foreign country, the gold would also be easily transferred by the bank into local currency with no care of the US dollar state. Gold is gold people.

Find a local family doctor, dentist, pharmacist and hospitals near the town you would end up in. It is quite common for expats and tourists to use these services when in the country. Go in and meet them. Understand procedures and how they accept payments.

Make a plan to travel. How would you get there? Costs? Have that cash on hand in your home and more. If you could not get there by plane what are your secondary options? Vehicle? Relocating to a new country is going to a last resort situation so plan for a secondary route.

Only repeated visits and eventually longer stays will get you truly comfortable and assimilated into a foreign culture. Have fun while you learn about your potential host nation. There is a big world out there. Don't rule out the future scenario where you have to leave home and set up a new life abroad.

Chapter 8.

Social Commentary: The colonists.

In the 17th century, England was a powerful nation/kingdom, and many could say well on It's way to being the dominant empire in the world. England was a beautiful land with rugged ocean crest landscapes and fertile valleys to grow food, build homes and start families. If all of this is true, then why did a certain group find England inhospitable? Why would a group, Puritans as they are called now, leave mother England to risk their lives at sea for months and fall upon the rocky shores of a new world, North America?

This very question is why I wrote this chapter. How could a group find within themselves the need, desire, and mandate to trek across the oceans, towards a new life? It was a task that meant almost certain death for most, if not in the travels, but in the first few years of life in the new world. The resolve to begin a new life, a life they controlled and not to be controlled by an oppressive government, must have been incredible.

The reason that so many of England's citizens risked their lives to leave their homeland and venture far across the globe in search of a new world was freedom. In the 17th century, King Henry VIII challenged the power of the Roman Pope and empowered the Protestant Church in England. The Puritans were neither true Catholics nor Protestants but instead believed in their form of the Christian religion that put God above all.

The Puritans, seeing that conflict in England was between two groups, of which they did not associate or agree with, decided it was time to leave. This is not much different than the division in Europe today. The rise of an immigrant culture that believes in Islam and Sharia law over western style democracy and the rise of far left-wing socialism has left many hard working and responsible citizens to feel abandoned and used. Again, the split of a nation between two groups that have isolated a smaller more determined sect has caused a migration outward.

Many in Europe today have decided that they will move themselves, their families and their money out to other nations. Not necessarily friendly or passive nations, but ones that would allow them to exist as they see right and not in an oppressed environment. They flee an environment where they feel unaccounted for or non represented.

I make this analogy, not for political banter, but to show that even today, people are willing to leave their birthplace to seek freedom. The idea of freedom is not naïve; many realize the dangers that will befall them in their new country. They leave despite the dangers. To live without freedom, without free speech, without representation is unacceptable. Without these basic freedoms, are we living at all? Are we member of our nation or an outsider already?

Let's look at another analogy. During World War II, the United States began drafting young men into combat. When this began, a small group of US citizens in Pennsylvania and Delaware, the Amish, who did not believe in taking up arms, refused to accept their draft notices. The men of this sect were in many cases imprisoned. At the end of the war, they were released. Upon returning home, the Amish families realized the United States no longer represented them. They were outsiders.

An interesting point to bring up here is that these Amish were and still are the closest relations to the original colonists that left England for America in the 17th century. They have not even changed their way of life from that time! How fascinating that they would again decide to move, despite all dangers and odds, to a new world. They chose Haiti, in search of a new life. A life in which they could respect themselves and decide how they would live and die. Not an oppressive government or a military-industrial complex.

Today, the decedents of the Amish that fled the United States for the island of Haiti still live and thrive in the original Amish, and many could say Puritan way of life. Who knows, in 50 years, the government of Haiti could be overthrown by an oppressive communist regime, once again sending the Amish families to venture far away in search of...freedom. Freedom is worth it.

I have presented these two historical events to show that any nation, no matter how powerful and perceivably vibrant, no matter how economically strong, can be a prison for those who do not feel represented, or may even be oppressed, by the government. Even in modern times, we have seen the collapse of once thriving nations into the chaos of war and dictatorship. Syria, Venezuela, Egypt, Iraq, Brazil. The list goes on and on.

The chapter I wrote on expatriation may have seemed extreme to many, but to those who know their history, it is well founded. Plan and account for your exodus out of your current homeland. Just prepare. Think about what your deal-breaker will be. For me, it will be hate speech laws. Arbitrary and undefinable. The end of free speech is the end of America. Without it, I will take my chances abroad. Perhaps not aboard a three mast, wooden, sailing ship, but aboard a plane or by foot. The risk is worth it. Freedom.

Chapter 9. Checklists.

Everyday backpack.

Flashlight.
Water.
Protein bars.
Cell phone and charging cables, extra USB rechargeable power brick and headphones.
Medications and first aid kit.
Cash.
Duct tape, whistle, safety pins and hard candy
Water filter survival pen.
Knife and multitool.

Vehicle.

Everything from your daily backpack prep: Water, protein bars, cell phone extra power brick, protein bars, medications, cash, knife, and multitool.
 Well stocked first aid kit including burn gels and wraps.
Water filter survival pen and a crushable, plastic water carry bag.
Flashlight and batteries.
Wool blankets and reflective material "space" blanket.
Gas siphon.
Gas can.
Escape tool, window smasher, and seat belt cutter combo.
Shovel, folding type is good
Fire extinguisher.
Extra oil and coolant.
Spare tire and jack.
Solar charger for the battery.
Small transistor radio with batteries and a headphone jack.
Toilet paper.
Emergency shelter, tent.
Gas masks for each family member.
Hiking shoes and a spare set of outdoor clothing.
12 volt to 120 volt inverter.
Fold up bike.
Camouflage tarp with tie down cords.
Misc. items: Jumper cables, bungee cords, a roll of duct tape, rope, toolkit and electrical repair kit, gloves.

Home "Hunker Down" kit.

Everything from your daily backpack prep: Water, protein bars, cell phone extra power brick, protein bars, medications, cash, knife, and multitool. Just keep them in your daily backpack, at the ready, to flee the house if need be.
Water. Case per person.
Water filter survival pens for each family member.
Water carry bags.
Water Desalination.
Food. A case of canned person.
Protein bars.
Coffee.
First aid kit with advanced items for burns, broken bones (splint kit) and eye injuries.
First aid and other family/emergency medical information books.
30 day supply of hygiene products, toilet paper. Baby wipes.
30 days of pet supplies.
30 day supply of prescription medications.
Fire extinguisher.
Multivitamins, chewable.
Flashlights, LED lamps and batteries.
Battery operated or hand crank rechargeable radio.
Cell phone and all chargers, power bricks.
Personal/portable power pack with inverter and outlets.
All important documents in a waterproof container.
Duct tape, bungee cords, heavy trash bags, several 1'X2" boards.
Sewing kit.
A handgun in locking, quick access case.
Extra ammunition.

Second handgun.
Long gun, rifle, shotgun.
All firearm repair and cleaning supplies, documentation, and holsters.
Less than lethal protection. Pepper spray. Expandable Baton.
Cord, rope.
Whistles, air horns.
Bright orange plastic tarp
Writing supplies and notebook.
Items to secure the door. Shims for under the door, wood, nails, hammer.
Warm blankets, towels.
Vodka. Small 1oz bottles best.
Gas.
Gold coins, Min $10000. In safe, but in a sturdy cloth bag to transport.

First aid kit for the Home.

Adhesive bandages (various sizes)
Liquid bandages(optional)
Antibiotic ointment and/or antiseptic wipes or spray
Sterile gauze (in rolls and pads)
Cold compress (have instant ones available, and also keep reusable ones in the freezer)
Hydrocortisone ointment
Calamine lotion
Rubbing alcohol
Hydrogen peroxide

- Hand sanitizing gel
- Eyewash solution (with eyecup)
- Sterile saline solution
- Sunscreen (at least SPF 15)
- Sunburn relief ointment
- Cotton balls
- Cotton swabs
- Disposable medical gloves
- Ace bandages
- Thermometer (get one appropriate for age of user)
- Bulb syringe
- Medical dosage spoons
- Blunt tip scissors (for cutting gauze and medical tape)
- Tweezers
- Fine needle (for helping remove small splinters)
- Save-a-tooth system (for preserving knocked out teeth so they don't die before dentist can put them back)
- Fever and pain reducers
- Antacids
- Nausea medication
- Anti-diarrhea medication
- Oral electrolyte solution
- Mild laxatives
- Antihistamines
- Cold and/or flu OTC medication
- Cough medicine
- Prescription medicines (only for family members with prescriptions)
- First aid instruction booklet (see below for suggestions)

Notification of any family members with allergies, in case emergency personnel need to come assist
Contact information for family doctor, dentist, and emergency contact numbers for family members; home, work, cell.

Chapter 10. FIRST AID BRIEF

You should have first aid kits, and books staged in your home 30 day "hunker down" kit. I want you to read over these basic ideas and get familiar with them. Consider this your first aid brief.

I realized when writing this book and discussing the various ideas within with family and friends that we rely far too much on the internet and emergency services to take care of us in any situation. I don't expect you to be an emergency medical technician here, I don't want you to freeze or panic when faced with a serious injury or similar scenario.

Allergic reactions.
The most serious allergic reactions can cause anaphylaxis. This reaction occurs minutes after exposure and, if left untreated, can lead to loss of consciousness, respiratory distress, and cardiac arrest. Signs include skin reactions such as hives, itching, or pale

skin, wheezing or trouble with breathing, lightheadedness, dizziness, or fainting, facial swelling, nausea, weak and fast pulse. Emergency care for anaphylaxis: See if they have epinephrine (adrenaline) auto-injector and help them if needed. Try to keep the person calm. Help the person lie on their back. Raise their feet about 12 inches and cover them with a blanket. Turn them on their side if they are vomiting or bleeding. The sooner the person gets their epinephrine, the better. The auto-injector comes with a single dose of medication to inject into the thigh.

Burns
Minor burns appear red and swollen. Unless they involve a large portion of the body, you can treat these at home by first washing the area with cool water for several minutes, covering the area with a sterile bandage or cloth and using an over-the- counter pain reliever.
Moderate burns are intensely red in color and will begin to blister. Follow the same first aid procedures as for minor burns and seek medical attention.
Severe burns may be charred black or dry white. Nerve damage may result in no pain in the most severely affected areas. Remove the patient from the source of the burning without endangering yourself. Remove any smoldering clothing and jewelry which may still be hot or may cut off circulation when hands and feet swell. Cover the burned area with a cool/moist sterile bandage or cloth. Do not apply any creams, ointments or ice, and do not break blisters.

Cold Emergencies

When exposed to very cold temperatures, the skin and underlying tissues may freeze. Frostbite is most common in the extremities - hands, feet, nose & ears. First, get the patient indoors or otherwise out of the cold. Then, places hands under the armpits to warm them slowly. Cover nose or ears with a clean, dry, gloved hand. Do not rub the areas. If they remain numb, seek medical attention. If you are unable to get immediate help, use warm (not hot) water to help rewarm the affected areas.

Choking
If the person's airway is only partially obstructed, they will still be able to speak short sentences and cough. Encourage them to continue but do nothing else. However, if the airway becomes completely blocked the person will not be able to speak or cough and will need your help. Stand behind the choking person and wrap your hands around their abdomen. Make a fist with one hand and place it just above their navel. With your other hand, grasp your fist and press in and up with a quick, forceful thrust until the obstruction is relieved.

Cuts or puncture wounds
Stop the bleeding by pressing a gauze pad or clean cloth against the wound. This is called direct pressure. Once bleeding stops, clean the area with mild soap and water, dry gently with a clean cloth (do not remove the dried blood) and cover with a protective bandage. Securing the wound with tape and stitches may be a last resort but could keep the wound from reopening.

Infection of wounds
Keep an eye on cut and burn injuries for these signs of infection such as increasing redness around the wound, yellow or

greenish-colored pus or cloudy wound drainage, red streaking spreading from the wound, increased swelling, tenderness, or pain around the wound, fever. Treating infections: Wound cleaning may be done with soap and water to wash away germs and decrease the risk of infection. Antibiotics help fight or prevent an infection caused by bacteria. NSAIDs, such as ibuprofen, help decrease swelling, pain, and fever.

Diabetes

If a person's blood sugar level drops too low, they will start to become confused, weak and eventually unconscious. As long as they are still conscious, able to sit upright and swallow, give them sugar cubes, chocolate, a non-diet soda or fruit juice, milk or peanut butter and jelly sandwich. If the patient becomes too weak to sit or swallow, or becomes unconscious, do not place anything in their mouth. Instead, place them on their side.

Electrocution

Even small amounts of electricity can be deadly
And even just a small mark on the skin could hide a serious internal injury. If possible, turn off the source of the electricity. If that is not possible, separate the patient from the electricity using a non-conductive material such as a plastic or wooden stick. Treat any burns.

Eye Injuries

Impaled objects - Do not attempt to remove the object. Instead, surround the object with large bulky dressings so that the object does not move. Cover both eyes. Even if just one eye is injured, the two eyes move together and can cause further injury. •
Foreign debris - Debris such as dirt, sand, and sawdust can

cause blinking and tearing which will help push the substance from the eyes. If the object remains, turn the head to the side and flush with water from the bridge of the nose letting the water run off of the opposite cheek.

Heat Emergencies

Heat exhaustion is characterized by weakness, a rapid heartbeat, low blood pressure, nausea and cool, clammy skin. Loosen or remove clothing and the patient drink cool (not cold) water or a sports drink. Avoid carbonated beverages. Afterward, have the patient lay down and elevate their feet.

Heat shock is characterized by hot, dry skin, a rapid heartbeat, rapid, shallow breathing and confusion or unconsciousness. Get the patient into a cool area. Cover with damp sheets and fan air over the patient to help cool the body.

Poisoning

Poisoning can be accidental or intentional and can be through contact (by ingesting, inhaling, injecting or touching) with a dangerous substance or simply having too much of something that is normally safe. If you know what poisoned the patient, follow the instructions on the container. Do not induce vomiting unless instructed to do so. Do not use water unless instructed as some poisons will react with the water to create something even more dangerous.

If cell phone service is available, the American Association of Poison Control Hotline is 800-222-1222.

Seizures
Try to keep the area around the patient clear of any objects that could injure further. If possible, loosen tight clothing. Once the seizure ends, try to have the patient lay on his or her side and reassure him or her. Do not put anything in the patient's mouth, whether to protect the tongue or food or drink. Do not restrain the patient.

Chapter 11. Emergency resources:

Apply for help after an emergency, immediate emergency advice:
https://www.disasterassistance.gov

American Red Cross Shelter system:
https://nss.communityos.org/cms/node/1

Passport resources:
Phone: 1-877-487-2778/ 1-888-874-7793 (TDD/TTY) Customer service representatives are available: Monday- Friday 8:00 am to 10:00 pm Eastern Time.
Email: NPIC@state.gov. Most email inquiries are answered within 24 hours. Please call for the status of your passport.

Travel planning, foreign laws, tips, dangers:
https://travel.state.gov/content/passports/en/go/checklist.html

Free language resources for traveling:

Fodor's Travel Phrases app
Sites:
DUOLINGO
LIVEMOCHA
BUSUU
LIVING LANGUAGE
FOREIGN SERVICES INSTITUTE
MEMRISE
BBC Languages

First aid guides, sites:
http://www.webmd.com/first-aid/
Save this .pdf on your laptop:
http://www.redcross.org/images/MEDIA_CustomProductCatalog/m55540601_FA-CPR-AED-Part-Manual.pdf

Firearms laws:
https://www.nraila.org/gun-laws/state-gun-laws/

Share this book.

Be willing to communicate with those you care about. Tell them how you feel about possible terror attacks, natural disasters, the possibility of moving to another city, state or even nation if need be.

Share this book with them. It could be an important part of preparing your whole family.

The Positive Mindset.

I want to leave you with a feeling of courage, preparedness and an overall positive outlook on your life. Right now your day to day survival means finding the most important element of life, happiness. As you prepare for the worst, live life to its best. Do not let depression or anxiety consume you. Live a life that is full and rich with love and respect for others.

Call your family, hug your kids and kiss your spouse as often as you can. You are now "that prepper" member of the family or friend circle. They will roll their eyes and listen to your stories about half priced sales on duct tape and weekend trips to the shooting range. Smile and be thankful for them, for one day, they will be thankful for you.

About the author.

Christopher LaVoie has served his country as a US Navy diver as well as his local community as an officer in the Honolulu Police Department. He has served on the Special Weapons and Tactics unit and worked as a federal counter-terrorism firearms/tactics instructor for years.

Christopher is the author of three earlier books on Hawaiian history, sustainability and his service in the US Navy.

Christopher is a fellow of the Pacific Center for Strategic Studies as well as avid outdoorsman and martial arts enthusiast. He has no social media at the time of this books printing, by design, but can be reached via email at urbanprepperbook@gmail.com.

CPSIA information can be obtained
at www.ICGtesting.com
Printed in the USA
LVHW041335140819
627619LV00028B/1471/P